Passive Income:

BEGINNER'S GUIDE TO PROVEN ONLINE BUSINESS STRATEGIES

(BOOK 6 OF THE SERIES "HAPPY JOB HUNTING")

ETHAN POWERS
(About The Author)

I0478621

HAPPY JOB HUNTING SERIES BOOK
Other related books on your career are:

Book 1 - Common Interview Questions
(Contains more than 100 model Q & A and the psychology behind the questions)

Book 2 - The Unspoken Interview Question That ALL Interviewer Will Ask
(Learn how to answer the nonverbal question which is extremely critical in all interviews).

Book 3 - Office Politics 101
(Discover why you cannot avoid office politics and actionable tips on handling the political game.)

Book 4 - How To Get Promoted 101: Forty tips you wish you knew
(Accelerate your promotion with these easy but powerful tips.)

Book 5 -Secrets Of A Highly Successful New Manager: Costly mistakes to avoid
(Master simple yet powerful strategies to change from doing work to managing work.)

<u>Table of Contents</u>

Introduction

After working for a couple of years, you may be feeling discontented and start to wonder if you should go into business. The majority of people will have this idea in their mind at one point in time. It may be a mid-career crisis, or being laid-off, or wanting to earn more money or just the desire to have financial freedom.

This book provides a safe path or a low-risk way to transition from being an employee to being an entrepreneur. Learn to earn passive income first until your passive income can easily exceed your monthly salary. Only then should you consider to quit your fulltime job.

Being an entrepreneur requires skills that are often the opposites of what you need as an employee. For instance, as an employee, it is not advisable to make mistakes, as your boss or colleagues will be quick to gun you down for the errors. However, as an entrepreneur, you are bound to make mistakes as you try out new strategies to horn in the best way to earn money.

The ideas presented in the book are the common strategies that newcomers tend to explore. I have tried them all with some degree of success.

Read the entire book, then at the chapter on "Action time", do take some action to get your feet wet.

Let's begin with the simplest idea....

Chapter I: Affiliate Marketing

Affiliate marketing is a company's method of product selling which signs up affiliates (individuals or companies) who do the marketing work in exchange for a commission.

You can see affiliate marketing in two perspectives: You can either offer your affiliate program to other people, or you can be the affiliate of another business.

As a business:

If you are the business offering the affiliate program, you will compensate affiliates with commission every time they generate a sale or lead on your website. If this is the case, your objective is to discover affiliates who are capable of reaching customers, especially in markets which haven't been tapped into just yet.

An important thing to remember is to NOT compete with your affiliates. For instance, if you are using certain channels (content sites, email lists, search engines) then these shouldn't be tapped into by your affiliates anymore. In this light, it is a must to come up with a binding affiliate agreement.

If you have any business partners, they should be made aware of such restrictions as well. Keep in mind that the program is yours, so you will be the one making and imposing the rules. Another option many take is to let the affiliates themselves run the entire marketing end.

As an affiliate:

What if you are on the other end? Being an affiliate has one goal: to earn some revenue for yourself. To do this, you must be able to put the needs of your customers first. Ask yourself what kinds of products and services can peak their interest. Once you've determine these, then that is the time to join affiliate programs for those products.

An affiliate program can help you boost your sales without upfront costs. However, it does require ample time and effort in coming up with a good marketing strategy. Be sure to choose business partners who can have the most impact for your goal.

Affiliate marketing is beneficial for those who want to sell products but don't have a store or a dealership. You don't need to put in investment money. Plus, you can earn revenue simply by sending the customer to the vendor. In the vendor's point of view, this is an advantage because he doesn't have to pay the affiliate unless any business was actually brought and made. In all cases, it's a win-win situation for both sides.

To get an idea of how much money revolves in the world of affiliate marketing, know that ten years ago - in 2006 - affiliates from all over the globe earned a whopping $6.5 billion. For each year that passed since then, this number only grew even more.

The Pros of Affiliate Marketing

- You can get started easily - in order to be an affiliate, you just have to pick a product to sell, sign up with the corresponding affiliate program, and place the tracking code on your site. For every sale made through your site, you'll earn money.

- You don't need special skills - don't fret if you have zero marketing education or background. Even if your selling skills are bad, you can still earn from the program. The only real skills you need are those that you already have. Just run your website as you normally do. Write and post content as you normally would. Leave all the transactions, sales, and legal brouhaha for the vendor to worry about.
- There is zero upfront cost - when you sign up with a program, you don't need to put in any investment money. You are purely banking on your skill and time. This makes everyone a good candidate for affiliate programs. Even if you don't succeed, you wouldn't lose anything.
- Earn from multiple sources - after a while, you'll surely be adept with the entire process. During this time, you

can use your skills to other areas. It is possible (and common) for affiliates to work with multiple affiliate programs from different companies (as long as the products are not competitors).

- Passive and automatic income - if you have successfully tapped into a sizeable audience, you can actively relax. Watch as your income grows passively whenever a sale is made through your site. After setting everything up, you can work whenever you want to and without even leaving the comforts of your own home.

The Cons of Affiliate Marketing

- You have no control over affiliate programs - if other brands and competitors are giving better products or offering better prices, you can't do anything about it except wait for the vendor to make some changes (if he wants to). It is also possible that you are selling and offering the same thing as thousands of other affiliates, so you really need to work hard to stand out.

- There is a lot of competition - the advantage is being able to join an affiliate program easily and quickly, however it comes with a downside as well: it also is as easy and quick for *others* from all around the world to become affiliates in the same program. This makes for tough competition, and many affiliates are very skilled in marketing and SEO, which gives them a big edge.
- You are paid for every sale - this is an advantage for the vendor, but a disadvantage for you. You only get paid if a sale is made on your site. This means that while you may be able to increase traffic for the vendor, if he loses business because his offer is bad or his product isn't good, then you don't earn anything as well.
- Your pay is shared - there are middlemen in affiliate programs. When you earn money, part of it is shared with the affiliate network

itself. This is how affiliate programs earn in exchange for the service of linking vendors with affiliates and providing tracking and reporting tools. This nature also reduces any direct communication that you can have with the vendor.

The disadvantages highlighted here can easily be resolved through **direct partnership**. This allows affiliates to partner directly with vendors, cutting out the middleman and ultimately getting more revenues for themselves.

How to Get Started with Affiliate Marketing

Affiliate marketing lets you recommend other companies' products or services in exchange for commission whenever a sale is made. In order to track this, a tracking link is used. This link contains a unique code that has been assigned to your website. Whenever this link is clicked on and buys something from the vendor's site in a given timeframe, a commission is earned.

Customers will pay exactly the same price for the products regardless if it was through an affiliate link or not. But the vendor will pay a fee to its affiliate for referring and generating the sale.

Choosing Affiliate Programs

The easiest way to land on an appropriate program is to check directly on the vendor's website if they are selling the products you want to promote. This is, of course, assuming that your website's content is already related to the products or services that you want to sell. Make sure that what you're selling is based on the interests of your audience.

Joining Affiliate Programs

When joining a program, you should never have to pay to become an affiliate. Both signing up and promotion of products are 100% free opportunities. If an affiliate network or vendor is asking you for upfront costs or any investment fees, be aware - you are just presented with a scam and you need to stay away from it.

Think of affiliate programs as free business opportunities. Even though the signup process will cost you nothing, you will have to make some expenditure along the way. These costs will be put into other tasks: running your website, promoting your blog, or using marketing tools (should you choose to) to assist you in being successful affiliates.

Earning Passively through Affiliate Programs

So the big question is: Is it possible to earn passive income by being an affiliate? Technically, the answer is Yes and No.

Yes - affiliate marketing can create a passive income stream. However, the "passive" part often comes only after putting in years of dedicated work. This comes true once you've already established your name and your website or blog as a credible source of information, and once you've amassed a hefty following from your target audience. You can have more than one site earning passive income, but before reaching that point, it'll take a lot of effort and time to build.

No - not every website reaches the point where it can generate passive income. A lot of sites need regular maintenance, even though the revenue generated can be enough to pay for this maintenance (instead of doing it yourself).

Important Points on How to Succeed with Affiliate Marketing

Experts in this field are able to generate five-figure monthly incomes. However, merely 1 to 5% of all affiliates and marketers reach this level.

This means that while it's possible, it is definitely no walk in the park. So how do you do it?

These three traits are musts in order to be exceedingly successful in affiliate marketing:

- Perseverance
- Patience
- Continuous education

Combined with prime strategies (discussed below), these traits can give you the secret on being a wealthy, successful affiliate:

1. **Choose a unique niche** - don't try to sell everything at the same time. Focus on one niche, on one market. Instead of scattering your time and efforts on multiple niches, concentrate on just one - but work on it and sell it well.

2. **Use marketing tools and techniques** - after completing everything else, the next step is to MARKET. Pay-per-click tools are often used by affiliates; however, it is best to stick to organic traffic and rankings (especially in the beginning).
   If you can't do it on your own, you can hire SEO agencies or professionals. Although you'll have to pay them for their services, you will have better organic results for your page and you won't have to

resort to PPC engines. You should only use PPC if you are already proficient with it. Otherwise you might end up being counterproductive and lose your profits.

3. **Become a valuable resource to your audience** - take the time to be an expert on the products that you are offering. This lets you tap into a wider foundation of information that you can write or talk about. This instantly builds up your credibility, which leads to trust. Unless your audience trusts you, then you won't be making any generated leads or sales from your website. Do some research on the science and psychology behind high-converting website content and design, which should benefit your goals.

4. **Work with various vendors.** This minimizes any trouble you might have if a particular offer or product does not convert well, or if one vendor does not pay you properly. This way, you reduce risk and

ensure that you still have some business to fall back to on whatever happens. Diversifying is a good strategy to cushion the blow. Just remember to focus on one niche - even if you have different vendors.

5. **Keep yourself updated with latest trends.** In the world of marketing, anything goes. What might be the standard today may not do so well tomorrow. Stay on top of things. Be assertive, too. Keep on seeking knowledge and expertise about the field. If you want to succeed in affiliate marketing, you need to allocate some time and energy into reading, researching, and embracing changes as they come.

6. **Persist and persevere.** No true success happens overnight. Even in affiliate marketing, where there are a lot of advantages given to you (no investment cost, instant start, minimal loss risk) - you can't possibly be the most successful marketer if you give up as soon as an obstacle presents itself.

Keep tracking your numbers and see which ones are working for you (and which aren't). If necessary, throw out non-converting products and replace them with better ones. Most of all is to be patient. If you are perseverant, it won't be soon before you begin cashing in on all of your efforts.

Affiliate marketing carries with it a lot of promise. If dabbled with properly - with gusto, patience, and persistence - it can be worth your while. By following the points mentioned earlier, you can find yourself at the front of the pack. Soon enough, you'll reap the rewards of investing your time and energy into this passive income stream.

Chapter II: Network Marketing

Network marketing refers to the business model where a distributor network presents the business opportunity. This also is often referred to as **multi-level marketing**, which refers to the nature of the business where payouts take place at more than a single level.

This method of income has gotten a lot attention from people searching for part-time sources of income. Popular US network marketing names include *Avon, Tupperware,* and *Mary Kay Cosmetics.*

The Pros of Network Marketing

- You can share products that interest people - health or weight loss products are great examples. Stories of successful weight loss are popular online, especially on social media. This shows how passionate people are about a certain niche - and you can tap into this passion. Because of the interest that's already there, you can effectively sell your product.

- You get an opportunity to make ends meet - a lot of network marketing opportunities come with low upfront costs and low-risk investments. You get initial products (or services), which when sold, can immediately earn you some money.
- Your time is yours - network marketing makes working from home a dream come true. No real marketing needs to be done outside of being a good representative for your product. Most often, network marketers start out with their family and friends until they meet and make more connections over time. Plus, majority of these products have already made their name in the market, so they are already established. These eliminate the need to hard-sell and advertise.
- You can have simultaneous streams of income - network marketing allows you to earn through direct

sales, downline commissions, and different performance bonuses. This means that even if it has been years since you've recruited someone to join, you can still continually profit off of their sales in the long run.

- You experience excellent mentorship and leadership first-hand - the environment in most network marketing businesses is one of friendship and leadership. When you sign up, you'll have a sponsor (or mentor) who will guide you as you build your name. Over time, you'll have more sales and commissions - and at the same time, your mentor earns as well. It's a win-win situation, even for the customers because they get satisfactory products.

The Cons of Network Marketing

- Majority of network marketers don't get rich - the truth is simply that not all who join these business opportunities get rich doing just this. Because there are no territorial restrictions with most organizations, you'll have to be the most competitive product representative if you want to get all of the business, which your fellow reps are also eyeing for.

- Face-to-face meetings dominate the field - only a low portion of all network marketing sales take place online. About 8 out of 10 sales happen on actual, face-to-face meetings. So if you're an introvert, this might be some problem. For this reason, a lot of reps sell to their friends and relatives and then just stop there.
- You need to be really patient - network marketing needs time for your success to grow. Look at it this way: as an independent product rep, you're practically working with your own business, because you can promote and sell whichever way you want to, whenever and wherever you want to. You have your own

business *without owning* the business.

As you sign up, they will give you free promotional materials, free mentorship, and other resources - but the bottom line is that the products won't sell themselves. You are there to make them known to others and convince them to purchase them. Having a solid presence and reputation as a network marketer will take a lot of time and patience, just like any other form of business would.

- Be prepared for a LOT of rejections - you will soon experience hearing lots of No's, especially in the beginning. On average, first-timers will have a 1% conversion rate. To put that into perspective: 99 out of 100 people you try to sell to will turn you down. If you are easily discouraged, you'll be out of the game sooner than later.

- You need to keep watching out for scams - it's tough to distinguish between actual opportunities and scams. Generally, having a concrete product that is being sold is a good sign that the opportunity is legit. However, if you're being asked for a sign-up fee and you are given nothing (but information) in return, you should turn away and not look back.

How to Get Started in Network Marketing

Follow these steps to get started with this passive income opportunity.

1. Do your research and learn all you can about this business. This will let you be geared without knowledge to determine real opportunities versus scams.
2. You'll need to fill out forms with personal and contact information with your chosen business network. Be prepared and expect their call.
3. If you're already aware of who your mentor is (or if a friend, relative, or acquaintance recruited you), you

can ask for their guidance through the signup process. It's part of their job and it shouldn't take long.

4. After joining, know that it doesn't stop there. Get moving right away. You did - you are now your own boss, but this comes with responsibilities. The amount of productivity (and procrastination) that you achieve is entirely up to you.

Important Points to be Successful with Network Marketing

The following points can enhance your network marketing, direct selling, and recruiting efforts.

1. **You need to be knowledgeable and realistic at all times.** In order to achieve success, be sure to study every step before you take it. Research about your prospective companies carefully, compare them from others, and weigh out the good

and bad of each company. This is important in finding a good match for you. Also, the more you know about network marketing in general, the better your odds are at avoiding failure, because you'll already know which mistakes to avoid. Plan your business strategy ahead of time.

2. **Find a good match.** Finding a good company and mentor is critical to your success. You need to find a product that you'll actually want to use personally. This makes it easy to sound proud and confident about the product you're representing. One last thing you need to be vigilant about the company's compensation plan and rates. Unless it's favorable to you, keep looking.

3. **Be respectable and ethical.** It's no secret that direct sellers and network marketers have a negative reputation in general. This is because a lot of their reps resort to creating false hype and using deception to bring in more recruits. As a result, many are led to believe that everyone in network marketing

behaves this way, which can be hurtful for those who are genuine and ethical in their ways.

Always be honest when dealing with customers and when recruiting. Having a product that you personally like will show off genuine enthusiasm on your part - and that's as organic as marketing can ever get. Do good business and never trick anybody - in the long run, you'll have a sound list of colleagues and customers who will stick with you.

4. **Determine your target audience.**
   A common mistake done by marketers is selling and promoting to EVERYONE, including friends and family. The industry gets it wrong with this way of thinking. In any other business, success is more tangible if there is a target demographic. Focus your marketing and selling to this target.

   Don't waste your time and energy on anybody who is clearly not interested with your products. If you're selling health and wellness products, a good market will be gym and fitness buffs, people recovering from illness or major treatment, and the elderly.

5. **Put in daily effort.** There is no overnight success with network marketing. It's perfectly fine to focus on recruiting new members - this is a good way to earn revenue instantly. However, the bulk of your income (if you're doing networking legitimately) comes mainly from direct selling.

Highly satisfied customers are potential recruits - they may even become leaders in the business sooner than later. Be sure to put some effort into getting the word out about your product one way or another every day. Need ideas? You can share a free sample product to your target audience, you can host a product launch or party, or you can post photos or videos on social media.

6. **Don't be a recruiter - be a mentor.** Your ability to bring in new people to the business not only

helps them find a source of income. It also helps you profit off of their business. While many perceive this as merely "using others", the truth is that nobody is being taken advantage of.

Both parties are rewarded in the process. They get a new business opportunity and you profit of their sales. However, keep in mind that their success is partly dependent on how you mentor them. This is not quantity over quality - you don't need to recruit dozens of new people in. The important thing to do is to **lead and train**.

Focus on their road to success; help them out the way your mentor helped you out when you were just beginning. Spend time answering their questions, motivating them, celebrating with them when they accomplish something, and be a friend when they encounter pitfalls.

7. **Be a good party host.** A big part of networking is hosting parties or presentation. While some think this is all about drinking coffee or

sharing a meal socially with other networkers, the truth is that these are avenues for business presentations. This is a good way to practice face-to-face dealings with current and future customers.

Plan your presentation well. Find out how to best showcase your products and the business in general. If you are successful, you might not just get new business - you may **retain and sustain** long-term, continuing business.

8. **Be a good listener.** One mistake that you can blindly commit is to make it all about yourself. Just like a bad date, nobody wants a talkative rep who is unstoppable with his presentation. Be sure to listen to your customers. What do they want? What do they need? What are they confused about? What are their fears about getting into this business? Before pitching a sale, answer their queries. Listen to them. This way, you can "tailor" your sales pitch to cater to their personal needs. Make it so that you and your product (or

business) is the SOLUTION to their problem. This way, they see that you're helping them, too, and not just selling some products to them.

9. **Be a unique representative.** Without a doubt, there will be thousands of other reps selling the same products that you do. This is a big challenge. How can you convince prospects to do business with you - and not with the many others? You need to dig deep and find some leverage to make you unique and stand out from others.

10.   **Always follow up with customers and prospects.** This doesn't equate to annoying and pestering anyone. A follow-up can make or break your relationship with a prospect. Sales depend heavily on **timing**. There are some cases when a person may tell you *No*, but this doesn't always mean *Never*.

If you were rejected once but you sense a hint of interest, there must've been something in your conversation which makes them want to get in business with you in the future. For cases like this, it's good to follow up with an e-mail (or you can simply ask for their e-mail address and add them to your mailing list).

Keep these pieces of advice in mind if you're thinking about entering the network marketing world. It's tricky and difficult at first, but if you are patient and if you work hard, you can be one of those who are able to generate income passively - and live off of it - through this means alone.

Chapter III: Stock Market Investing

Over the past century, some of the wealthiest people have become rich by investing in stocks. In fact, majority of the names who have made the Forbes 400 list own huge shares in private and public corporations. The stock market has been around for decades, and while it has produced incredible success stories, not everyone who invests in it ends up wealthier. It is important to understand how the market works, its advantages and disadvantages, and some tips of the trade in order to make better decisions.

The Pros of Stock Market Investing

- The returns are higher over the long run - since 1926, the stock market has had an average of 10% returns per year. This outperforms most of the other assets available. Although the returns can vary each year, if you look at them over a long time period, they can give out double-digit returns.

- You are allowed to diversify - this is diversification in terms of your assets. Doing so reduces your risk, should one investment collapse. This way, you don't wipe out your whole portfolio. You can buy stocks from different companies and sectors, and this is a great hedge to protect your investments.

The Cons of Stock Market Investing

- You can lose money - the fact is, even if the market performs well over the long run, companies still go bankrupt. This leads to plummeting share prices. Also, you can make a mistake when buying or selling at a bad time, which will lose you money instantly.
- You need to wait for stock prices to recover - in stocks, prices constantly

go up and down depending on a lot of factors. However, the prices DO return to their previous price even after plummeting down. The wait is variable, but it may take years for this to happen. Individual stocks can recover more or less quickly than the market average, too.

How to Get Started in Stock Market Investing

You need to learn about the ways to invest money and the types of assets that you can own.

5 Ways to Invest Your Money

1. You can invest through your 401k plan
2. You can invest through your 403b plan if you work for a non-profit
3. You can invest through a brokerage account
4. You can invest through an IRA account

5. You can invest through either a dividend reinvestment plan or a direct stock purchase plan

5 Types of Assets You Can Own

You can own these assets either directly or using a pooled structure (mutual funds, exchange traded fund, hedge fund, or index fun):

1. Common stocks - you get an ownership stake from an actual operating business when you invest in stock. You also acquire your share of its resulting dividends and net earnings. Stocks (or equities) have produced the most wealth and have been the source of the highest number of returns (among different assets) over the previous centuries.
2. Preferred stocks - these are special kinds of stock which usually give higher dividends. It has, however, a limited upside.
3. Money markets - these investments are highly liquid. They are meant to "protect" your purchasing power.

You can see them as a cash equivalent. Money markets come in varieties and alternatives, too.

4. Bonds - bonds come in the form of corporate, savings, municipal, and even government treasury bonds. These are used when lending money to companies, institutions or businesses, municipalities, or countries.

5. REITs - these are real estate investment trusts, especially designated by companies. At the company level, these allow zero taxation if the shareholders are paid with over 90% of the earnings. Usually, the assets are invested in property and real estate projects.

Important Points to be Successful in Stock Market Investing

1. **Identify your goals.** What are your long-term goals? Why do you want to invest in stock? Are you going to want your money back in a few

months, a few years, or longer? Will you use the earnings for retirement, for your kids' college expenses, to buy property, or to have something to leave to your beneficiaries once you're gone?

Setting your goals clearly is important, because if you're likely to want your cash back in just a couple of years, you may want other kinds of investment. The stock market is very volatile, which means you cannot be certain if your investment is fully available whenever you need it.

2. **Know how much risk you can take.** Risk tolerance refers to your feelings toward risk - how anxious do you get in its presence? Psychologists define it as the degree to which you choose to risk going through a less desirable outcome in pursuit of a more desirable outcome. For instance, are you willing to risk $1000 to win $10,000 - or would you rather invest $1000 and get $1000 in return? Risk tolerance has a lot to do with genetics, but studies

confirm that it is influenced by income and education. The more wealth and education a person gets, the more they can tolerate risk. Consequently, it is negatively affected by age (the older you get, the lower your risk tolerance is). Humans have varying risk tolerance - there is no right level whatsoever. This tolerance is also affected by your own perception of the risk itself. For example, if you lived during the early 1900s, you would've been called a daredevil if you rode a car or got on a plane - but doing these things today are considered normal and safe.

On the other hand, riding horses would've been seen as completely ordinary back then - but people today will feel less comfortable with it, since most of us are around horses all the time. In this light, perception is very crucial - and this applies well in investing stocks.

As you learn more about the market (how you buy and sell, how much price change is happening, how easy you can liquidate an investment), you can see stock investing as less risky than you did when you first started out. As a result, you may be less anxious during investing - even if your risk tolerance has not changed because your perception has.

3. **Keep your emotions in check.** Your biggest enemy in this market is not being able to control your own emotions, so much so that you can't create logical decisions. Company prices can be perceived here as the "combined emotions" of its whole investing community. If a big percentage of the investors are worried about it, the company's stock price will likely plummet down, but if the investors are optimistic about the company's future, then its prices are likely to rise.

In market lingo, someone who feels negatively about the stock market is called a **bear**. Someone who feels positively about it is called a **bull.** There is a constant brawl between bears and bulls during market hours

- and you can see this with the constant fluctuation of securities prices. Such fluctuations are often affected by speculations, rumors, and *emotions*, instead of analysis and logic.

4. **It is not a stock market - but a market of stocks.** This old adage applies to every investor, especially new ones. Before you invest, be sure to take ample time to study about the market and research on individual securities. Unless you intend to buy an exchange traded fund, you should concentrate on individual securities instead of the entire market.

   Very rarely does every stock have the same direction - even if the averages decline by more than a hundred points, company securities prices will still go higher. Be sure to familiarize yourself with these areas before making any investment:

   ☐ Technical terminologies and key metrics

- ☐ Methods of choosing stocks (fundamental and technical analyses) and timing
- ☐ Types of stock market orders (market orders, stop market orders, limit orders, stop limit orders, and trailing stop loss orders)
- ☐ Kinds of accounts you can invest in (cash accounts, margin accounts)

5. **Practice diversification.** Investors who are experienced will eschew diversification because they are confident that they've done all of the required research to quantify and identify their risk. Experts are often comfortable enough about their ability to identify all possible problems that may pose risk to their position. They are capable of liquidation before their investments even experience significant losses. Andrew Carnegie once said that the safest strategy in investing is to *"put all of your eggs in one basket and watch the basket"* - however, NEVER make the mistake of going in half-

cocked. Only experts with years of experience and millions of earnings under their belt can be this confident with stocks.

Instead, go the other way - the safe route - and diversify. It is wise to own stocks from various companies, in various industries, and even in various countries - if you can. This will give you a safety net that assures you that no single negative event can cause losses to all of your investments.

For instance, imagine having stocks from five separate companies. With each company, your goal is to keep profiting over time. However, circumstances will change inevitably. After a year, you may have two companies performing remarkably. Your other two companies from other industries are doing fairly well, too.

However, your fifth company experienced a major decline and had to be liquidated as payment for a big lawsuit. Because you diversified, you can recover from losing an entire investment (a fifth of your whole portfolio) - because of the performance of your other four companies.

Stock market investing has amassed significant returns over other investment forms. At the same time, it showcased its best features - easy liquidity, complete transparency, and proactive regulation. These all factor in to an equal, fair playing field for all who want to get into stock investments. This is a great opportunity for anyone who wants to build large-scale assets, as well as to individuals who are savers by nature.

You can succeed in this method of passive income if you are willing to spend significant time and energy in its learning process. With experience, you'll soon be able to properly manage your risks - and if you are patient enough, you will get to reap the fruits of compounding income, which is something only very few people get to experience in their lifetime. Keep the advice mentioned earlier in mind and you might just break into the big leagues sooner than later.

Chapter IV: Forex Investing

The foreign exchange (forex) market is where people trade currencies. Currencies are vital to all people in every country in the world - some may realize it, while others don't. This is because currency trading allows foreign business and trading to take place.

For example, if you are a U.S. resident and you want to buy wine from France, you - or the store where you buy it from - have to pay the French for the wine in euros (EUR). In this example, the U.S. importer has to exchange U.S. dollars into its equivalent value in euros.

This applies in other settings, too, such as traveling. An American tourist in Japan cannot pay for products or services using U.S. dollars - simply because that isn't the local currency. He goes to exchange his American money for the local currency - in this case, the Yen - at the exchange rate applicable for that day.

The necessity for currency exchange is the main reason why the forex market is the biggest and most liquid one in the world. Even the stock market is dwarfed by the size of it. The sum of daily trades change every time, because of various factors. The Bank for International Settlements reported that as of August 2012, the forex market had trades going up to $4.9 trillion per day.

The biggest aspect that makes forex unique is the fact that there are no central markets for it. There is no one place for all its transactions. Instead, exchanges are conducted over-the-counter, electronically. This means that trades are made through computer networks between traders all across the globe.

The forex market operates 24 hours in a day for five and a half days in a week. Currencies are exchanged globally in the main financial centers of New York, London, Frankfurt, Zurich, Singapore, Hong Kong, Tokyo, Paris, and Sydney. This encompasses almost all time zones. This means that when a trading day ends in Tokyo, the market starts anew in the United States. Because of this, the market is highly active round the clock, causing constant fluctuations in the price quotes.

The Pros of Forex Investing

- You get a lot of leverage - the market gives you leverage in your trades. Even having a small starting capital can accomplish a lot over the long run. There are even markets that let you have a 50:1 or 100:1 leverage ratio. This means that a single dollar that you own can be worth $50 or $100 during trading.
- You can trade round-the-clock - this is another advantage that isn't available in other markets. For more than five days a week, you can keep trading for 24 hours a day. You get to trade at whatever time that is most comfortable and convenient for you - except on weekends (standard time).
- There are fewer and lower fees - compared to the stock exchange, the fees are significantly reduced.

The fees are usually limited to the spread of the transaction (a spread is the difference in value between any two currencies which are being traded). This means that you need to pay less and save more.

- There are several tools and services available online - because forex trading can be done in the comforts of your own home, the tools related to it are also available online. These services have significantly lifted the burden off of traders, especially beginners. These assist in studying, tracking, and analyzing the market. You can begin trading with just a few clicks. If you are just starting out, it is wise to utilize and take advantage of all the tools available to you. Many of these are for free, and can help prepare you as you enter the world of forex.

- You can use automated software for trading - this software is able to do the transactions for you, of course dependent on how you've programmed it. This can help you trade at the right time and under the right circumstances. This is recommended for more advanced users.

The Cons of Forex Investing

- The market is volatile - this is probably the most popular downside of the forex market. It is fast and volatile, and even if this can work to your advantage (you can earn quickly), it can be dangerous just the same. You can experience losses quickly, since the value of currencies can fluctuate in a split second - it is very hard to predict if they will go up or down, making it difficult to decide where to invest your money.
- Leverage can be a downside, too - we mentioned about the advantage of having leverage earlier. However, even if you can invest bigger with a small capital, it can also result to far greater losses (larger than your initial investment). Think of it this way: if you can make $100 for each

dollar of your capital, you can also lose money in the same scale.

How to Get Started in Forex Investing

1: Be familiar with technical terminology.

- Base currency - the currency you are spending (transaction currency)
- Quote currency - the currency you are buying (counter currency)
- Exchange rate - how much you need to spend to buy another currency
- Short position - situation where you are buying quote currency and selling base currency
- Long position - situation where you are buying base currency and selling quote currency

- Bid price - the price at which you (or your broker) want to buy the base currency in exchange for the quote currency. This is the best price at which you will sell to the market.
- Ask price – the offer price. This is the price where you are willing to sell base currency for quote currency. This is the best price where you will buy from the market.
- Spread - this is the difference between the bid and ask price.

2: Learn how to read a currency quote. There are two numbers here: on the left is the bid price, and on the right is the ask price. For example:

USD/CAD = 1.2000/05

In this example, the bid price is 1.2000 and the ask price is 1.2005. Usually, the last two digits of the ask price are quoted. The bid price is always lower than the ask price - which is how you make money: buy low and sell high.

In this example, it simply means that to buy the USD/CAD currency pair, you will buy USD (base currency) in exchange for CAD (quote currency). Look at the ask price to see how much the market is charging for the USD currently. In the quote above, you will pay C$1.2005 to purchase $1.

To sell this pair (or simply, to sell USD), look at the bid price to see how much you'll get in return. In this quote, you'll get C$1.2000 for selling $1.

3: Choose which currencies you will buy and sell. By making predictions on a specific country's economy, you will be able to decide which ones to buy and which ones to sell. Factors to consider are the country's political situation, trading position, economic reports, GDP, inflation, and employment status. These all directly or indirectly affect the country's currency value.

4: Calculate potential profit. Learn how to do your computations.

> The change in value between 2 currencies is measured by a **pip**. Typically, a pip is equal to 0.0001 of a change in value.

> For instance, if you are trading EUR/USD and it moves from 1.547 to 1.548, then it means that the value of the currency increased by 10 pips.

> The next step is to multiply the pips changed in your account by the current exchange rate. The result will signify how much value has increased or decreased in your account.

5: Open a brokerage account. You can do this online, but first, be sure to do your research.

> - Compare different brokerages before opening an account. Choose one that has had years - even decades - of actual trading. Experience is very

vital in forex trading. Pick a company that knows what it is doing, so that it can take better care of you. Be sure that it is regulated by an oversight body. If a broker submits to government regulation voluntarily, you can be assured that it is transparent and legitimate.

- Choose what kind of account you're opening. You can go with either personal or managed accounts. With the former, you can execute your own trades. With the latter, a broker will make the trades for you.
- Accomplish all required paperwork. Today, paperwork can be filled out manually or through online forms, and you either request for physical forms through the mail or simply download them from the broker's site. Be completely sure to double-check how much it'll cost to

transfer money from your
bank account to your
brokerage account. These fees
will be cut from your profits
later on.

- The last step is to activate
your brokerage account. You
will receive an email with a
link to activate it. You will be
redirected to a page with
further instructions to help you
get started.

6: Start trading. Trading involves various
processes:

- The first step in trading is market
analysis. You can accomplish this
through various methods:
    A. Fundamental analysis - this
    involves examining the
    economic fundamentals of a
    country and using the
    collected information when
    making a trade decision
    B. Technical analysis - this
    involves using historical data
    and charts when deciding how

the currency will move. Charts are often provided by brokers and online tools.

   C. Sentiment analysis - this is the most subjective form of analysis. It involves analyzing the "mood" of the market to determine whether it's bullish or bearish. It's not always easy to determine the market's sentiment, but making a good guess can help in making trades.

- Identify your margin. This varies from one brokerage to another. Usually, you are allowed to make large trades even if your investment is small.
- Place an order.
  - A. Market order - you tell your broker to buy or sell with the current market exchange rate.
  - B. Limit order - you tell your broker to make a trade but only at a specific price. For example, you instruct him to buy currency after reaching a specific price or to sell

currency if it plummets down to a specific price.

C. Stop order - this is a decision to buy currency above the market price (often anticipating that it will increase in value in the future) or to sell currency lower than the market price (as a means to cut losses).

- Track your profit and losses. It may be tough, especially at first, but try not to be too emotional. This market is highly volatile - and you need to keep this in your mind when trading. There will be a LOT of fluctuations. The important thing is to keep studying the markets and implementing your strategy carefully. Tracking profit and loss can help you modify any strategies that might not be working - and to keep on doing strategies that are giving you a lot of profit.

Important Points to be Successful in Forex Investing

1. **Familiarize yourself with the markets.** Education is *very* important in forex. Be sure to allocate time every day to study different currency pairs and research about the factors that affect them. Do this before investing - and risking - your money.

2. **Practice makes perfect.** There are several practice (Demo) accounts available with most brokerages. Take advantage of these to hone your trading skills. These are great ways to see what it's really like when trading currencies without risking real money. Once you're confident with your abilities as a trader, then go out into the real world and start trading real money.

3. **Watch the markets' weather conditions.** If you are a fundamental trader, be sure to be updated with important news and events from different countries. If you are a technical trader, use

analysis tools and indicators to predict the movement of the market. Or, like most traders do, use both forms of analyses to improve the quality of your trades.

4. **Set limitations.** It sounds simple, but many traders fail miserably at knowing their own limits. This is a critical factor for your success in the future. Know how much you are willing to risk. Set your leverage (ratio) according to your needs. NEVER risk more than you can afford to lose, or else you'll end up with huge losses - and worse, you can end up bankrupt.

5. **Modify your strategy as you go.** While consistency and limitations are vital in this industry, there are times when you need to explore. Re-evaluate your plans - are they still in accordance to your needs? Chances are, over time, your needs have changed as well. Feel free to change your strategy as your financial status or goals change.

Chapter V: Property Investing

If you are interested in diversifying your assets beyond bonds and stocks, property investing can be a good opportunity. You have probably seen a reality TV show or two focused on flipping homes quickly (buying, renovating, and then reselling homes at a higher price).

The concept is exciting, but the truth is that **renting** is the true heart and core of property investing. This is because, through the course of decades, there really has been very little price appreciation with houses. On the other hand, renting can generate a steady cash flow every month - just like a classic utility stock that pays dividends. If you do receive price appreciation, that's just a small bonus.

However, investing in rental property isn't similar to purchasing a low-cost index fund. It takes a LOT of work, from selecting the right property, to managing and maintaining it, to dealing with tenants. You need to be absolutely certain that you're prepared for this kind of investment. You need to be sure that you will be able to put in time and effort into it.

Experts say that landlords need to be "handy" - you have to be capable of fixing things (and it helps if you actually like doing this). Be wary if you already have a full time job, or if you have kids.

The norm is to expect tenants who call in the middle of the night because something got broken, or tenants who don't pay rent on time, or to have maintenance issues with your property. If things go smoothly and you don't have many problems, consider yourself lucky - this rarely happens in this kind of investment.

The biggest mistake beginners make is underestimating the expenses related to renovation and maintenance. Being unprepared for these can quickly pull your money down the drain. Before getting into property investing, learn about the business as a whole - weigh out the pros and the cons - and be sure that you're

100% prepared (physically, mentally, and financially).

The Pros of Property Investment

1. It provides stability - owning or renting property is a stable form of investment compared to other markets. It has its ups and downs, but in general, it is a lot less unpredictable and volatile. This is because it takes more time to sell properties (unlike stocks, which you can sell in a split second). Also, property is always in demand.

2. You can take advantage of leveraging your investment - even if you start out with a low investment, you can buy a whole lot more. For instance, you can get a property loan from the bank. If you are approved, all you need to cash out is the deposit and you can begin developing your property. Take it into perspective: Say you have

$50,000. Instead of fully investing it on just stocks worth $50,000, you can take it together with the bank loan and buy a $300,000 property.

3. It is an opportunity to generate positive cash flow - this is possible through renting. If you collect enough rent, you can use it to pay for your expenses (mortgages, loans, utilities). Technically, you are having others buy the property for you. If you manage the property smartly, you can even have money left over, generating a source of passive income and positive cash flow for you. Once you fully pay off the mortgage, you'll have even more positive cash flow.

4. You can enjoy taxation benefits - you can claim tax benefits from owning property. For one, if you lose money on the property, this can be offset against your income - then you can secure a tax saving. Also, you can increase your tax savings by claiming depreciation on fixtures and fittings.

5. There is a potential for financial freedom in the long run - a lot of people are enthralled by property investment for this very reason. It *can* be a great long-term investment. Because no more land is being "made", you get to secure your portion of land in the present and benefit off of it in the future. As inflation progresses, your property will likely increase its value. As a result, rents will go up (as long as you choose a good property location). Over time, you can improve your cash flow by collecting more rent. If managed right, you can totally live off of your investment alone and enjoy long-term financial freedom.

The Cons of Property Investing

1. Liquidity can be a problem - while you can share stocks instantly, property will take longer to sell. It can take months to sell. This can be

a problem should you need to quickly liquidate the property or need the cash.

2. There are often issues hidden about the property - this is why it is very important to do your research beforehand. Be sure to examine your paperwork and to inspect the actual property yourself. Still, even with the most meticulous property buyers, there are problems that will pop up every now and then.
It is uncommon for a purchaser to acquire a property and merely sit back and relax right after. There are always problems that need fixing, tenants that need attending to, and bills that need to be taken care of.

3. You need a substantial amount to get started - some markets allow you to start investing with relatively low capital. In properties, however, you need *at least* thousands of dollars just to get entry. The bigger and better the property is, of course, the higher its cost will be.
Plus, the prices of real estate are constantly rising, making it more

difficult to break into this market. This escalating cost keeps a lot of potential investors at bay, leaving the opportunities only to those who have a lot of money in their hands.

4. Unexpected events can strain your cash flow - these include sudden vacancies and increasing interest rates. These pose a problem because property is a huge investment. You are left with a significant mortgage that you'll have to pay off. These unexpected changes can hurt your cash flow. If you are relying on the steady weekly income that you collect from tenants, it may be a problem when one of them suddenly moves out.

5. There is little diversity - having all of your eggs in one basket is common in property investing because of its high entry fee. This opens you up to a lot of risk, should the market suddenly change or should you experience unprecedented losses with the business. There isn't much to fall back to.

In order to safeguard yourself from this risk, you can do two things: (1) Specialize. Enhance your skills to the maximum level possible. The better you are skilled at property investing, the fewer risks you need to face and the more returns you can enjoy; or (2) Diversify. If you can afford to do so, be sure to invest in various markets (stocks, commodities, other businesses).

6. Dealing with tenants can be stressful - having "bad" tenants can directly affect you by not paying rent on time, but there are other ways they can be a nightmare to you, too. A lot of tenants take no regard for the property since it isn't technically theirs, and they often have a lot of complaints, even with seemingly mundane things. They can be both financially and emotionally stressful.

7. You'll need to cover recurring and unexpected costs - ongoing costs are a part of property investing. These include mortgage payments, maintenance and renovation expenses, insurance costs, and

council rates, among others. Plus, you never know when there will be damages or problems that need fixing out of the blue.

Hopefully, you'll practice enough proper planning to make your property investment worthwhile. Landing a good property and having sound management skills can let your rental income surpass all other expenses, and possibly give you a positive cash flow for years to come.

How to Get Started in Property Investing

1. **Check if you are financially prepared.** List all of your assets, incomes, and expenses. This will give you a clear picture on how much money you have that can be used for investing and on the expenses that you'll need to spend later on. Having a steady job and a good employment record will help

you get a loan easily. Don't cross off property investment right away - banks can help you out if everything checks out.

2. **Get pre-approved.** You can get this from your mortgage broker or from the bank you're loaning from directly. Having a broker can help you greatly if you aren't certain about your financial preparedness. A common misstep that a lot of first-time investors make is applying for more than one pre-approval. Remember that every time you file an application, the bank or lender will go through your credit record. If they see that you've got multiple inquiries, it becomes an automatic red flag, which substantially reduces your chances of getting pre-approved. A few things you can do to increase your odds are: checking your credit rating, reducing your existing debts, and finding out if you are a candidate for a loan.

3. **Have clear goals.** It helps to be certain on which goals you want to accomplish. What does success

mean to you? Generally, property investors get into this business wanting to secure their future financially, or to have financial freedom soon. To achieve your goals, you need to set concrete timelines on when you (realistically) want to accomplish them. From that timeline, work backwards.

4. **How do you feel about risk?** Understand your attitude and tolerance to risk. Understanding this helps create strategies on investing. This will give a clear picture on how much you're willing to risk (hence, lose) while chasing after something bigger. The more you risk, the more you can lose. But also, the more you risk, the more you can earn.

5. **Learn how to budget.** It's not the most fun thing to do, but it is a MUST. It ensures your ability to break even with income and expenditures. You'll be able to see where you're spending most of your money. If you need to readjust your budget, you'll know where to look

and which expenses to work on down the line.

6. **Make a purchase plan.** This plan will help actualize your goals of having more assets and growing your portfolio until you reach the point where you've met the income that you're shooting for. This plan acts as a blueprint - a structure - that aids you to keep yourself inside the lane.

7. **Be smart and informed.** This includes taking advantage of all tools available to you, understanding the market and its trends, and being vigilant and wary of scams and peddling schemes. The ability to do these will help you make better, informed decisions - which are essential when making big investment choices.

8. **Keep focused.** Remember that this is a logical, not an emotional, decision. It is business first of all. Remember to:
   - Be precise on your goals

- Set a clear timeline on when you want your goals to be achieved
- Properly identify milestones that need to be passed to get to your goals

Once you've accomplished these, you are ready to purchase your first property investment.

Important Points to be Successful in Property Investing

1. **Do your research.** There are very rare cases when investors jump into real estate investment without certainty and land with both feet still intact. These are the lucky few. It is wise not to push your luck, though. The wise way to get started is to do your homework, study the property you're eyeing, and make a reasonable plan on how you want to utilize it after acquisition.

2. **Connect with a network of investors.** This can be as simple as reaching out to local investors. You can casually hang out with them, ask them questions you may have, ask for advice if they are willing to give it. You can even have them show you around some of their investments. The more information you can learn from them, the better. Connect with investors from the same locality as you have a stronger grasp of what "works" in your area, which can be substantial. There are a lot of tutorials and articles online, but gaining actual, local understanding is far better in this sense.

3. **Understand the jargon.** Before you go off contacting investors, it's best to spend some time learning the technical speak. This way, when they start talking about cap rates, you won't have a blank gaze and look silly. Also, if you do engage in conversation and hear something you don't understand, don't pretend to be knowledgeable and cruise

along. Instead, ask them what it means - you'll come off as genuinely interested and you'll learn more as well.

4. **Trust basic math.** Don't walk away just yet - the math involved in property investing isn't as complex as calculus. It's leaning more towards fifth grade math, really. This isn't hard to learn. Basically, **cashflow = income - expenses.** For instance, buying a gallon of paint costs about $20. Hiring a painter, however, will cost about $200. Now, *this* is the kind of math you have to be good at. Never assume anything, instead, use basic math to ensure that every transaction and deal you make is 100% accurate and solid.

Property investing takes a lot - a huge capital, long hours, a lot of energy, planning, and preparation. If you're looking into investment that spans the long-term instead of the short-term, then it might be right for you. While it doesn't guarantee instant [positive] income right away, it can be a great opportunity to build yourself a portfolio that will allow you to generate passive income in the future. It can be substantial enough to quit your day job, especially if you've accomplished all of your set goals.

Chapter VI: Action Time

This is the chapter that will change your life. It is time for you to take action.

Get involve in affiliate marketing and network marketing. There are valuable lessons in these two fields that will sharpen your entrepreneurship skills. For example, in affiliate marketing, you will get to know that building a customer base is very important and for network marketing, you will learn how to be a leader or mentor.

For affiliate marketing, go to www.clickbank.com. Sign up, then click on the affiliate marketplace to find some products that would interest you. Begin promoting the product.

For network marketing, do join those that are online-based. Although business are conducted mainly online, you will still need to interact with people face to face. Find someone that you know to begin with. Do not start this purely by signing up online on your own. You will need some hand-holding for network marketing in order to be successful.

By now you will notice that for both ideas, online business is common. This is highly desired as opposed to doing business purely by the brick and mortar method.

Try out these two methods for at least six months before you jump to the other strategies. The main objectives is to gain experience, do not be too focus on the money making aspect at this point in time.

Alright, some of you are keen to try stock market trading or forex. Here is a powerful way to get you started. Open a binary options trading account and start trading after you have sufficient skills in technical analysis or fundamentals. The objective is to understand your emotions relative to money. Binary options is a good way to begin as it is low cost and you get fast feedback in your behaviour. Be warned though, most binary options websites are out to scam you. They will trick you to part with your money by giving you additional funding for "free". Or they will delay payment or other means to deceive you. Just bear in mind that you are trading binary options to sharpen your understanding of your emotions when it comes to money.

If you can stop trading when you have make profits or suffer losses according to your plan, then you can consider stock trading or forex. The key to being successful here is your emotions with money.

<u>Conclusion</u>

For you to be successful in any of the above strategies, you have to spend considerable time gaining experience. Just like the black-belt martial arts expert...you can demonstrate tremendous and amazing skill but not before years of practise.

Do not give up at the slightest obstacle. Keep going and you will succeed.

Do look out for additional books that I will be writing in the near future for in-depth tips on affiliate marketing or online related business.

If you need additional advice on the above strategies, feel free to write to me at ethanpowers2014@gmail.com. Be sure to write your email title as "Book 6 - more tips needed"

Good luck in your endeavours.

<u>One Last Thing</u>

I would be most grateful if you could kindly write a short review about this book as reviews are like lifelines for me, as a writer.

Thank you.

ETHAN POWERS

Author's Page